D1121974

CLASS IN AMERICA

THE AMERICAN
MIDDLE CLASS

BY DUCHESS HARRIS, JD, PHD
WITH REBECCA ROWELL

Essential Library

An Imprint of Abdo Publishing | abdopublishing.com

ABDOPUBLISHING.COM

Published by Abdo Publishing, a division of ABDO, PO Box 398166, Minneapolis, Minnesota 55439.
Copyright © 2019 by Abdo Consulting Group, Inc. International copyrights reserved in all countries.
No part of this book may be reproduced in any form without written permission from the publisher.
Essential Library™ is a trademark and logo of Abdo Publishing.

Printed in the United States of America, North Mankato, Minnesota
032018
092018

Cover Photo: Jirat Teparaksa/Shutterstock Images
Interior Photos: iStockphoto, 5; Red Line Editorial, 7, 19, 53; Shutterstock Images, 8, 12–13, 50–51, 52,
72–73, 78–79, 82; Daniel Krylov/iStockphoto, 17; Enrika Samulionyte/Shutterstock Images, 21 (top);
Danny Johnston/AP Images, 21 (bottom); Leemage/Universal Images Group/Getty Images, 27; AP
Images, 29, 41; CBS Photo Archive/Archive Photos/Getty Images, 32–33; Joe Scarnici/WireImage/
Getty Images, 34–35; Dariusz Jarzabek/Shutterstock Images, 38; Scott Stewart/AP Images, 43;
Wave Break Media/Shutterstock Images, 49, 88; Monkey Business Images/Shutterstock Images, 58;
Blend Images/Shutterstock Images, 61; Laura Gangi Pond/Shutterstock Images, 64–65; Jana Shea/
Shutterstock Images, 68; Bill Clark/CQ Roll Call/AP Images, 74; James R. Martin/Shutterstock Images,
77; Chris Maddaloni/CQ Roll Call/Getty Images, 91; Mandel Ngan/AFP/Getty Images, 96

Editor: Arnold Ringstad
Series Designer: Becky Daum

LIBRARY OF CONGRESS CONTROL NUMBER: 2017961016

PUBLISHER'S CATALOGING-IN-PUBLICATION DATA

Names: Harris, Duchess, author. | Rowell, Rebecca, author.
Title: The American middle class / by Duchess Harris and Rebecca Rowell.
Description: Minneapolis, Minnesota : Abdo Publishing, 2019. | Series: Class in America | Includes
        online resources and index.
Identifiers: ISBN 9781532114038 (lib.bdg.) | ISBN 9781532153860 (ebook)
Subjects: LCSH: Middle class--United States--Juvenile literature. | Lifestyles--United States--Juvenile
        literature. | Social classes--Juvenile literature. | Race relations--Juvenile literature. | Social
        classes--United States--History--Juvenile literature.
Classification: DDC 301.451--dc23

CONTENTS

ONE

THE MIDDLE CLASS
NO MORE

Melanie and Daniel Vega grew up in New York City. Melanie lived in public housing as a child. Daniel's mother raised him on her own as a single mom. She sometimes needed three jobs to earn enough money for them to survive.

As adults, Melanie and Daniel seem to be succeeding in the nation's most expensive city. They have two children and together earn more than $100,000 a year. The couple and their kids live in Spanish Harlem, a neighborhood in Manhattan. The Vegas live alongside many other Puerto Rican families. Melanie and Daniel pay $3,000 per month for their three-bedroom apartment. Melanie had expected their apartment building to

Spanish Harlem, also known as East Harlem, is one of many places in the United States where rents have risen dramatically in recent years.

be a high-quality place because of the cost to live there, but the environment has made her think otherwise:

> You know, you walk in, and either it's weed smoke or pee that you smell. You don't want to come home to the place that's your sanctuary, and you have to write this fat check every month. And it's, like—this smells like a bathroom.[1]

The Vegas also worry about the safety of their neighborhood. Melanie walks the couple's 11-year-old son, Jacob, to school. It is only four blocks, but she and Daniel do not want him to walk alone.

National Public Radio (NPR) journalist Ari Shapiro spoke with the Vegas about their experience. He asked Melanie if she felt middle class. She said, "I don't think so."[2] Having shelter is a basic need. Without it, feeling safe is difficult. In the United States, a lack of affordable housing has long been an issue for the poorest people. But the scope of the problem has widened. In some US cities, many people who are in the middle class are facing the same trouble. New York is one of those cities.

Various people and groups, including economists, use different numbers to define the middle class. Using data from the US Census Bureau as a starting point, in 2014, the Pew Research Center set the income range for a middle-class family of four as between approximately $48,000 and $145,000 per year.[3] Melanie had just started her own business, adding more money to the

AVERAGE ANNUAL INCOME
BY OCCUPATION AND CITY, 2017

OCCUPATION	NATIONAL	NEW YORK	DENVER	DETROIT	LOS ANGELES
ADMINISTRATIVE ASSISTANT	$35,329	$45,702	$39,312	$36,002	$41,276
BUS DRIVER	$28,860	$46,867	$30,472	$28,948	$39,584
HIGH SCHOOL TEACHER	$50,298	$51,236	$42,033	$44,746	$61,010
NURSE	$64,503	$84,129	$57,162	$57,381	$80,343
POLICE OFFICER	$45,535	$67,347	$55,462	$36,171	$64,638[4]

Salaries for an occupation can vary greatly across the United States, and they may not be enough to pay for high housing costs and other basic needs.

The typical middle-class vision of homeownership in a suburb is out of reach for many people who might once have considered themselves middle class.

family's $100,000 annual income, which moved the family higher in the middle class. But Melanie does not feel middle class: "I think when we think about what middle class would be like, we would think they would be a little more comfortable."[5]

RETHINKING THEIR STATUS

Melanie's sentiments are shared by other Americans. Some Americans whose income would place them in the middle class have found themselves questioning whether they are actually middle class. This doubt comes from the struggles they face. Middle-class earnings do not always lead to a middle-class lifestyle. These people are not achieving the American dream. This ideal includes things such as owning a home, buying a car, paying for children's college education, and going on vacations. Such things are often associated with the middle class. But for many people whose income falls in this range, these acts are often aspirations or hopes, but not reality. They remain only dreams.

Achieving these long-term financial goals is often challenging, and some middle-class Americans do not have money available for unplanned expenses. Shapiro asked Daniel Vega about having money for an emergency, such as a car repair. Vega explained that he rarely feels like he is prepared for such an expense. He said, "It's always in the back of my mind."[6]

RICH RENTERS CAUSE RENT HIKES

Americans are renting apartments more and buying houses less. New York University's Furman Center analyzed statistics from 2006 to 2015 for rental housing in metropolitan areas with at least one million residents. The analysis revealed that wealthy households, or those earning more than 120 percent of the area's median income, increased as a percentage of renters.

The demand for rentals has increased, particularly in the most popular metropolitan areas, where rents are already high. The study reported that rents increased between 2012 and 2015 in most of the 53 metropolitan areas studied. Knowing their apartments are in demand, landlords often increase rents. The spike in the number of wealthy apartment seekers has caused even sharper rent hikes. The result is that people who are not wealthy have an increasingly difficult time finding affordable housing. Report coauthor Sewin Chan explained, "The rise in higher-income renter households may mask the significant housing affordability challenges faced by lower-income renter households. [They] are both struggling to pay rent and have fewer affordable options if they need to move."[7]

Vicente Barredo has lived in the El Barrio neighborhood of New York City's East Harlem for 50 years. Shapiro spoke with Barredo about the neighborhood and his experience, asking whether Barredo thought of himself as middle class. Barredo responded, "That's a good question. I think I used to be middle-class, but right now I don't think about that question."[8]

BELOW-AVERAGE INCOME, ABOVE-AVERAGE RENT

In 2016, the median income for a family of four in New York was $53,000. This amount was lower than the national average. In contrast, the cost of living in Manhattan, where the Vegas live, was more than twice the national average. The result is that middle-class New Yorkers are trying to pay for more with less.

Patricia Redden has lived in her New York apartment for nearly three decades. She is able to afford it because it is rent controlled. The rent has a legal limit. The landlord cannot ask for more than the limit. If her rent reflected the typical rates landlords are charging today for apartments that are not rent controlled, she could not pay it.

HOUSING CRISIS

Financial advisers often suggest spending approximately 30 percent of one's monthly income on housing costs. The Joint Center for Housing Studies found that 21.3 million US renters exceeded that amount in 2014. Of those people, approximately 11 million spent at least 50 percent of their income on housing.[10] Both of these figures were record highs. Paying for housing has become particularly challenging in cities such as New York.

The challenge of putting so much money toward rent is that

MOVING IS NOT THE ANSWER

Some people suggest that Americans who struggle to pay rent should move to a less expensive place. Writer Hanna Brooks Olsen disagrees. She notes that moving can have far-reaching effects. Most police officers do not live in the cities where they work because they make too much money to qualify for housing assistance, but too little money to pay the high rents. Many white officers who work in large, diverse cities instead reside in suburban areas with little racial diversity. Olsen reflects, "In the conversation surrounding police tactics and violence, having a police force that actually represents the community they serve is crucial to curb implicit bias."

Olsen also suggests that society should address rent increases as part of addressing poverty. She explains, "If we want people to be less dependent on social services—and to no longer struggle to pay rent—we have to let them live [in] places where there is opportunity."[11]

New, expensive luxury apartments have contributed to pushing lower-income people out of the neighborhoods where they have long lived.

it makes less money available for other expenses. These include food and clothing, which are immediate needs. Middle-class Americans end up sacrificing future needs as well. With less money available, setting aside savings for emergencies, major purchases, and retirement ends up becoming impossible. Housing researcher Dan McCue explains, "When you have to dedicate such a high proportion of your income to rent every month, it forces you to make difficult decisions."[12]

Edward Goetz, professor of urban and regional planning at the University of Minnesota, commented on the situation the Vegas and other middle-class Americans are experiencing: "I think that for many people, the housing crisis that middle-income New Yorkers are feeling right now has been a depressing and recurrent way of life for decades."[13]

According to Goetz, affordable housing units have disappeared by the hundreds of thousands. They have been demolished or made into high-cost housing. Goetz adds that these problems have been gaining more public exposure as more people are affected by them.

For now, Americans like Tsee Lee continue to struggle. The New York City teacher earns $54,000 annually and worries not only about getting by today but also about his financial future. Lee described his situation: "I don't feel middle class. I don't have enough disposable income left over after I've paid all my monthly bills. I am putting some money aside for retirement, but I'm sure not spending on vacations."[14] Lee noted that people in many professions once had a higher standard of living than they enjoy now:

> There's a myth that the US economy increasingly requires high levels of education or specialized skills, but everyone from auto workers to sanitation workers to professionals like teachers [once] did well, whatever their résumé showed.[16]

AMERICANS FEEL POORER

Americans today are feeling poorer and less affluent than they actually are. A 2014 Pew Research survey found that 40 percent of respondents reported being lower middle class or poor, but only 32 percent of them were, according to standard economic measures. In addition, 44 percent said they were middle class, and 16 percent said they were wealthy. In reality, 26 percent were wealthy.[15]

For middle-class Americans, this is no longer true. Middle-class America has changed. It has shrunk and continues to decrease in size. Its members are earning at a slower rate than in the past and at a slower rate than other Americans. Meanwhile, the wealth of companies and rich citizens continues to grow. The idea that if you work hard, you will achieve and succeed—the American dream—is not as certain as it was only a few decades ago. This new reality has dimmed the outlook of many middle-class Americans. For many of them, the American dream seems as if it may never become a reality.

DISCUSSION STARTERS

- What do you think about the Vegas' experience? What do you think about landlords raising rent because demand is high?

- Have you heard of the American dream? What do you think it is? Where did you hear someone talking about it?

- How is housing related to the American dream?

TWO

DEFINING THE
MIDDLE CLASS

A merican society is commonly divided into social classes that are roughly defined by wealth. One of the simplest representations of social classes includes three categories: poverty, the middle class, and the upper class. There are no universal definitions for the divisions. However, both the US government and independent researchers have developed dividing lines between these classes to help them study the makeup of American society.

AMERICA'S LOWER AND UPPER CLASSES

The US government has defined one income level: poverty. This is the lowest income level. In 2017, the poverty level was

One way to define people in the middle class is by the places they can afford to live and the products they can afford to buy.

described as an annual income of $18,871 or less for a family of three. The figure was $24,257 or less for a family of four. Americans in this economic class struggle to meet basic needs. The US Census Bureau has estimated that approximately 14 percent of Americans, or approximately 43 million people, are in the lowest financial class.[1]

At the other end of the spectrum is the upper class. This class does not have a standard definition by the US government. People have different ideas of the upper class. The phrase *the top one percent* has become a common way to refer to the wealthiest Americans. US tax data showed that to be in the top one percent,

NATIONAL INCOME REPORTING

Each September, the US Census Bureau gives a report on income in the United States. In addition to reporting the median income, it provides the mean, or average. The Census Bureau determines this number by adding together all incomes reported and then dividing that by the total number of people. In terms of US income reporting, the mean is generally greater than the median. The difference is a result of some people having extremely high incomes. These incomes greatly outbalance the low incomes and distort the results to give a false sense of income equality.

The Census Bureau provides annual income data for three groups. One data set is income per person for Americans age 15 and older. Another is family income, an average for related people living under one roof. The third is household income. This average is for all the people living at the same address. The people do not have to be related. The Census Bureau also sorts income data by age, education, and race.

AMERICAN INCOMES, 2017

HOUSEHOLD INCOME RANGE	MILLIONS OF HOUSEHOLDS	PERCENTAGE OF TOTAL (APPROXIMATE)
LESS THAN $15,000	14.1	11.2%
$15,000-$24,999	12.1	9.6%
$25,000-$34,999	11.9	9.4%
$35,000-$49,999	16.3	12.9%
$50,000-$74,999	21.5	17.0%
$75,000-$99,999	15.5	12.3%
$100,000-$149,999	17.8	14.1%
$150,000-$199,999	8.3	6.6%
$200,000+	8.8	7.0%[2]

No matter what income level is used to define the American middle class, many millions of households fall into the middle class category.

an American in 2014 had to have an annual income of at least $465,626.[3]

MIDDLE CLASSES AROUND THE WORLD

Roughly two billion people worldwide belong to the middle class. Each year, they spend almost $7 trillion. Latin America has had the greatest growth in the middle class. This growth has made a difference on multiple levels. Individuals are able to live better. Businesses are providing more services. And countries are less reliant on their neighbors for assistance, making them more independent.

AMERICA'S MIDDLE CLASS

The US government also does not define the middle class. However, the US Census Bureau identifies median income. This is the income that is in the middle of the highest and lowest incomes reported by Americans. That means half of Americans earn more than the median, and half earn less. In 2015, the median household income in the United States was $57,230. The figure rose to $59,039 in 2016.[4]

Public opinion on the definition of the middle class varies. In some polling, a majority of Americans have said middle-class income is less than $100,000 per year for a family. In a 2013 Allstate/National Journal poll, the greatest percentage of respondents said a middle-class family would earn $50,000 to $74,999. That same year, the University of Connecticut asked people to identify the upper income limit for a family of four to be middle class and provided five options: $29,000; $49,000;

A studio apartment in an expensive area, such as New York City, *top*, may cost the same as a large home in a different part of the country, such as Arkansas, *bottom*.

$79,000; $139,000; and $180,000. The greatest percentage of respondents, 36 percent, chose $139,000. The next highest was $79,000, with 30 percent of responses.[5] The study demonstrates how definitions of the middle class can vary considerably.

Raw income data can give a sense of class divisions in America, but such numbers are an inexact measure. Each person's situation plays a role in his or her economic success. Various factors can affect that situation. These include having children or other caregiving responsibilities, suffering a death in the family, getting married, finding a place to live, and getting a job. Journalist John Yemma discussed the middle class in 2015:

> *Middle-classness is not uniform. A middle-class income in New York City gives you a very different lifestyle than it does in Pocahontas, Ark. Family structure makes a difference, too. A single mom with a middle-class income has to pedal much faster than does a middle-class empty nester. And, of course, every individual's experience differs. A teacher, a book, an unexpected opportunity, an inner drive—all can alter a life's trajectory.[6]*

PEW RESEARCH STUDIES THE MIDDLE CLASS

The Pew Research Center has developed its own definition of the middle class, based in part on the median US income. According to Pew, a middle-class income ranges between 67 percent and

200 percent of the US median income.[7]

However, Pew's numbers do not line up exactly with those of the Census Bureau. The research center works to adjust for the variations in life situation that can affect a person's economic success. To adjust for higher and lower costs of living in different parts of the country, Pew uses Census Bureau data. A person making a specific income might live well in one city and struggle financially in another. For example, someone who lives on an income of $50,000 in Minneapolis, Minnesota, would need to earn more than $85,000 to live similarly in San Francisco, California.[8]

Pew also considers marital and family status in its income ranges. In 2014, middle-class individuals earned $24,173 to $72,521, middle-class couples earned $34,186 to $102,560, and a middle-class family of four earned between $48,347 and $145,014.[9] By accounting for location and marital and family statuses in its calculations, Pew provides a comprehensive range

OTHER DEFINITIONS OF MIDDLE CLASS

Different people and groups describe differing annual income ranges as middle class. Aaron Pacitti, assistant professor of economics at Siena College, defined $39,764 to $64,582 as the middle of the middle class. Robert Reich, professor of public policy at University of California, Berkeley, described the middle class as earning between $25,000 and $75,000.[10]

WEALTH, CONSUMPTION, AND CLASS

Many Americans have a relatively meager income and still live well. They have amassed wealth over time. New York University professor Edward Wolff has studied wealth and defines someone with a net worth greater than $400,000 as wealthy. Using wealth as the determiner of class, the top fifth are considered wealthy, and the lowest fifth have little wealth or are in debt. The remaining three-fifths are the middle class.

University of Notre Dame professor James Sullivan focuses on consumption to determine class. Consumption includes spending on housing, transportation, and entertainment. Based on consumption, he describes Americans who spend $38,200 to $49,900 per year as being in the middle class.[11]

of numbers to help Americans understand whether they are middle class.

VISIONS OF THE MIDDLE CLASS

Beyond the pure numbers different organizations use to identify the middle class is the lifestyle that comes to mind when people think of the middle class. Americans have different visions of middle-class life, and these visions have changed over time.

A 1991 poll by *Time*, CNN, and the research firm Yankelovich asked Americans what things a middle-class person would be expected to have. In 2012, the University of Connecticut conducted a similar poll. The responses had changed significantly in 21 years, with the percentages declining across the board. In 2012, about 45 percent (down from 70 percent in 1991) believed a middle-class person would own a home. About

37 percent (down from 46 percent) thought a middle-class person would have a college education. And about 28 percent (down from 41 percent) expected a middle-class person to own stocks, bonds, or other investments.[12]

The idea of a prosperous American middle class had originally developed in the years following the US victory in World War II (1939–1945). In some ways it came to define the nation, representing the reward for hard work and good citizenship. But by the early 2000s, the American middle class, once an iconic part of US society, had changed significantly.

DISCUSSION STARTERS

- How would you define the middle class? What things are needed for a middle-class lifestyle?

- When thinking about the different income ranges used to define the middle class, which one seems the best? Why do you think so?

- Have you heard the phrase *the top one percent* used to describe wealthy people before? In what context did you hear it?

- What is income? What is wealth? How are they different?

HISTORY OF THE
MIDDLE CLASS

The notion of the middle class has long played a major role in US history. People—both Americans and non-Americans—often identify the United States with the middle class. Many immigrants moved to the United States in search of a better life. They envisioned the American dream: if you work hard, you will succeed. This idea of hardworking, prosperous people with good values came to represent the American middle class.

THE GI BILL

The modern American middle class developed after World War II. The United States and the rest of the world had just survived a long period of economic struggle known as the Great Depression

The idea of traveling to America, working hard, and achieving a better life has long been part of the American dream.

Vast new tracts of suburban homes sprang up in the decades following World War II.

(1929–1939). Then, after Japan's bombing of Pearl Harbor, Hawaii, on December 7, 1941, the United States officially entered the war, which had started in 1939. For the places where the war's battles were fought, in Europe and Asia, the conflict was enormously destructive. Whole cities were flattened by land and air attacks.

Unlike countries such as the United Kingdom and France, the United States emerged from the war with little damage to its infrastructure. Following the US victory in 1945, the nation entered an economic boom period.

One factor that contributed greatly to the formation of the American middle class was the Servicemen's Readjustment Act. Commonly referred to as the GI Bill, because soldiers were often nicknamed GIs, the law was created in 1944. With it, the US government created opportunities for military veterans by providing job training, money for school, low-interest loans to buy a home

MADISON'S MIDDLE CLASS

James Madison wrote the first drafts of the Bill of Rights and the US Constitution and served as the fourth president of the United States. In 1792, he wrote about the citizens of the newly established United States of America, including the middle class. He noted the importance of this group:

> The class of citizens who provide at once their own food and their own [clothing], may be viewed as the most truly independent and happy. They are more: they are the best basis of public liberty, and the strongest bulwark of public safety. It follows, that the greater the proportion of this class to the whole society, the more free, the more independent, and the more happy must be the society itself.[1]

The residents of Levittown had to follow strict rules. According to Barbara Kelly, curator of Long Island Studies at Hofstra University, Levittown's contracts for leasing and buying included "all sorts of subtle and not-so-subtle rejoinders about how to live like middle class people."[3] Levittown had rules about mowing grass, hanging laundry, and painting in certain colors.

Levittown also had a race rule. William Levitt created a covenant for his town. One rule, clause 25, banned "any person other than members of the Caucasian race." This applied to residents. Minorities were allowed to live there only if they were servants.

In 1949, war veteran and African American Eugene Burnett experienced the racism of Levittown when he tried to apply to buy a house there. The salesman he spoke with would not let him, explaining, "It's not me. But the owners of this development have not yet decided to sell to Negroes."[4]

or start a small business, and unemployment income.

War veterans took advantage of these new benefits in huge numbers. Home construction skyrocketed from 114,000 new houses in 1944 to 1.7 million in 1950. During this time, some of the biggest housing projects in US history were built. In 1947, William Levitt made 4,000 acres (1,600 ha) of land in Long Island, New York, into the nation's first subdivision. It was the beginning of the suburbs. The development was busy. Workers built 30 houses a day, and each lot had a tree in the front yard. When the project was finished, Levittown had 17,000 houses.[2]

MIDDLE-CLASS NORMS EMERGE

The development of houses was quickly followed by a rise in the purchasing of consumer goods. Americans began buying more cars. Then they needed to outfit their new houses. The new suburban backyard was a great place to cook, so barbecues became popular. As television became an essential source of news and entertainment, screens began appearing in more homes.

This era created a culture of buying that became the standard of American behavior. And the middle class became the subject of popular television shows. Real middle-class Americans could watch fictitious middle-class Americans in series such as *Father Knows Best* and *Leave It to Beaver*. These programs represented an idealized home life of the era. The father worked and brought in the money. The mother stayed at home and cared for the house and children.

Author Peter Barnes discussed the American middle class in his book *With Liberty and Dividends for All*. He described the middle class of the 1950s and 1960s:

THE MIDDLETONS

In 1939, the manufacturing company Westinghouse had a film created for the New York World's Fair. In the film, a family named the Middletons visits the fair. They tour the Westinghouse Building and experience the latest technology meant to make life better. The exhibit shows the future of middle-class life. The Middletons, as their name suggests, are supposed to represent middle-class Americans. In one scene, a dishwashing contest takes place. One woman has a Westinghouse dishwasher. Her rival washes dishes by hand. The first woman wins, highlighting the benefits of having an electric dishwasher.

Sitcoms such as *Leave It to Beaver* portrayed an idealized vision of middle-class suburban life.

The quarter century after World War II was the golden age of America's middle class. Twenty million veterans went to college or bought homes thanks to the GI Bill. Green-lawned suburbs sprouted like mushrooms after rain. Families filled their garages with cars, tools, and barbecues.[5]

Another new development of the 1950s, the credit card, helped make it easier to purchase all these new goods. Unlike previous forms of credit, which were limited to a single store or business, credit cards could be used at a wide variety of places. Americans could buy things on credit and pay for them over time. They could also build up credit card debt. In September 1958, Bank of America introduced 60,000 credit cards in Fresno, California, for testing. The card became Visa, and within ten years, Americans had more than 100 million credit cards.[6]

TELEVISION'S
"MIDDLE CLASS"

Television has depicted the middle class differently over time. The era of the 1950s and 1960s "was particularly escapist" according to NPR's TV critic, Eric Deggans.[7] The 1950s show *Leave It to Beaver* was one example. The family lived a comfortable, suburban lifestyle.

Similar shows continued into the 1970s, with series such as *The Brady Bunch*. But television in the 1970s also presented working-class families in shows such as *All in the Family*. The 1980s brought more change. *Roseanne* portrayed a middle-class family differently. Roseanne's family struggled financially, reflecting the reality that many middle-class Americans lived daily. Roseanne's family was not one for viewers to aspire to be like. Instead, it was one many viewers could relate to.

However, this was not the case for all middle-class Americans. Minorities saw few people like themselves on television. In the late 1960s and early 1970s, Diahann Carroll provided the only middle-class African American on the air as the lead character in *Julia*. Middle-class families of color have been slow to appear on television. Perhaps the best known is the Huxtable family of *The Cosby Show*, which premiered in the 1980s. Depictions of middle-class families have become more varied in recent years, with the Mexican American Suarez family on *Ugly Betty*, the African American Johnson family on *Black-ish*, and the Taiwanese American Huang family in *Fresh Off the Boat*.

Randall Park and Constance Wu star in *Fresh Off the Boat*, which began airing in 2015.

These cards helped Americans buy the goods that retailers and the media promoted as necessary to maintain a middle-class lifestyle.

THE MIDDLE CLASS TODAY

In the 2010s, middle-class Americans have some things in common with those of the postwar era. They may own a home and seek out the latest in consumer goods. But lifestyle expectations have changed. Today's middle class is expected to have more than the middle-class households of the 1950s and 1960s.

Homes of today's middle-class Americans are larger. The square footage of new homes has risen more than 50 percent over the last half century. Air-conditioning was once a luxury, but it has become a necessity. Middle-class homes regularly have multiple televisions, and people use them to enjoy

THE IMPORTANCE OF SOCIAL SECURITY FOR SENIORS

The Social Security Administration, the government agency that provides a basic income for retired Americans, publishes reports with statistics about the funds it provides. These reports show how critical Social Security benefits are to older Americans. For example, in 2011, 85 percent of single people and 87 percent of married couples who were 65 years old and older received these benefits.

The same report found that the program is crucial for many recipients' survival. In 2011, 64 percent of seniors who received Social Security benefits relied on the money for at least half of their income. Journalist Jonathan Peterson responded to that figure: "This is a reminder that Social Security is incredibly important for the middle class, as well as the less affluent—a basic, simple fact often overlooked in discussions about its role and its future. . . . Social Security income is indispensable for the middle class."[9]

Social Security plays an even greater role for seniors of color. While many white retirees have other financial resources, such as Individual Retirement Accounts (IRAs), many seniors of color do not. In 2014, Social Security was the only source of income for 18 percent of whites ages 65 and older. In contrast, it was the sole source of income for 26 percent of Asians and Pacific Islanders, 33 percent of African Americans, and 40 percent of Hispanics.[10]

video games, hundreds of cable or satellite channels, and streaming subscription services such as Netflix. In addition to utility costs such as electricity and water, people pay monthly for internet service and cell phone service. In their garages, current middle-class families expect to have two cars. This was not the case in the 1950s and 1960s, when one car was often considered enough.

The standard of living improved for the middle class from the 1950s into the early 2000s. However, this trend has begun to reverse for some people. Fewer people are considered middle class. Even those who are middle class may find it harder to keep up with the fast pace of consumer spending. Changes in the US economy helped bring about this change. One of the most dramatic shifts occurred in the late 2000s, with the onset of what became known as the Great Recession.

DISCUSSION STARTERS

- From what you read about Levittown, what were positives and negatives about it?

- Do any of the shows you watch on television or online show middle-class families? How are these families depicted?

- Why do you think some people have called the 1950s the "golden age" of America? Who might not call that period a golden age?

FOUR

AN ECONOMIC
CHANGE

The years immediately following World War II were prosperous. The US economy grew and grew. Businesses succeeded, which led to growth in workers' pay. It was a stretch of prosperity for the middle class that did not last.

STAGFLATION

America's golden age was the result of industrialization following the war. Many countries grew during this time. To some economists, this era lasted from World War II until the 1970s. This period saw the largest increases in wealth in the nation's history.

George R. Tyler, author of *What Went Wrong: How the 1% Hijacked the American Middle Class . . . and What Other Countries Got Right*, wrote about America's economy:

Auto manufacturing was one career that boomed in the years following World War II, only to decline in later decades.

Americans have long been proud of their economy. And why shouldn't we be? From the time we were children, we've been told that we live in the best country in the world, with the most expanding and dynamic economy. We've been told that our economy allows Americans to enjoy a lifestyle that is the envy of the world. And we've been told that we live in the home of the American dream, a country that—more than any other—allows people to rise up from poverty into the ranks of the rich.[1]

He goes on to ask whether all those things are still true, and then answers his own question: "Unfortunately, the answer is no. These things haven't been true for a long time. But they used to be true."[2] The decline began as the economy suffered in the mid-1970s. Inflation increased while economic growth stagnated. Economists refer to this combination as "stagflation."[3]

In 1980, Americans elected Ronald Reagan president of the United States. He implemented economic practices that became known as Reaganomics. The results were fewer rules and restrictions for businesses and lower taxes, especially for the rich. In addition, government spending increased quickly, particularly on national defense.

Average wages suffered during this time. They did not grow and sometimes even decreased, even as productivity grew. Only 5 percent of workers had enough gains to outpace the rate of inflation during that time. Those gains were primarily among

In 1982, auto and steel workers marched outside the White House in protest of Reagan's economic policies.

the top one percent of earners.[4] This worsened the existing gap between the wealthy and the middle and lower classes.

At the time, Reaganomics was often called "trickle-down economics." Lowering taxes on businesses and on wealthy people was meant to stimulate broader economic growth. It was theorized that this growth would work its way through the economy and benefit all citizens. Many economists, including Tyler, are skeptical of this concept. "Well," he explained, "thirty years on, most families are still waiting for trickle down to deliver."[5]

Workers have continued to face low wages. In 2011, Massachusetts Institute of Technology economist Paul Osterman reported on the issue:

> *Last year, one in five American adults worked in jobs that paid poverty-level wages. Worker displacement contributes to the problem. People who are laid off from previous stable employment, if they are lucky enough to find work, take a median wage hit of over 20 percent.[6]*

Regarding the practices of Reaganomics, Tyler wrote, "The United States simply made a fundamentally wrong turn. What could have been a temporary sidetrack became the main track— and American families are still paying the price decades later."[7]

THE GREAT RECESSION

The 2000s brought a major economic disaster. As the first decade of the new millennium progressed, the economy initially did well. In particular, the housing market soared. Banks gave home loans to people who really could not afford them, and then they sold the mortgages in a risky, elaborate system to earn more money for themselves. In 2007, a credit crisis began as borrowers defaulted on the home loans. That same year, the housing

THE EFFECTS OF THE INTERNET

Technology executive, investor, and author William Davidow thinks the internet is "playing a central role in wage stagnation and the *decline* of the middle class." He describes it as "a colossal economic disappointment." The problem, Davidow says, is jobs. Other technological advances, such as the integrated circuit, expanded the electronics market and launched new industries, including personal computers. The result was more jobs. The internet has had the opposite effect. Online shopping has led to the loss of retail jobs and a vanishing need for people to build retail stores. Davidow advises, "We had better get to work on searching for and implementing policies that will offset the internet's displacement effects."[8]

The internet has also given companies a new way to outsource work. Companies send some parts of their business, such as technical support and call centers, overseas. They save money, since wages in these countries are often much lower than in the United States. In 2016, the top five countries to which companies outsourced work were India, China, Malaysia, Brazil, and Indonesia.

market crashed and jeopardized the banks that held the loans. December 2007 marked the official start of the collapse that became known as the Great Recession.

The situation worsened as the months passed. Bit by bit, the economy declined. The credit crisis had affected the global economy and weakened it. Finally, in September 2008, the financial sector suffered a major blow when Lehman Brothers, the fourth-largest bank in the United States, filed for bankruptcy. The shock waves of this failure rippled through the economies of the United States and other countries. The stock market lost

AMERICAN RECOVERY AND REINVESTMENT ACT

Shortly after taking office as US president in 2009, Barack Obama signed the American Recovery and Reinvestment Act (ARRA) into law. Politicians created the law in response to the Great Recession. The goal of the legislation was to save current jobs, create new jobs, and spur economic improvement.

The ARRA's budget included $288 billion in tax relief and $224 billion for programs such as food stamps, Medicaid, and unemployment payments. An additional $275 billion was intended for education, infrastructure, and transportation. Within two and a half years, the Congressional Budget Office estimated that the number of Americans with jobs grew by 1 to 2.9 million as a result of the law.[12] Even with this growth, the unemployment rate remained high. ARRA's proponents used the job growth as evidence that ARRA was a good idea. The law's opponents used the continued high rate of joblessness as proof that ARRA was a bad idea.

almost half of its value from its peak in August 2007. The sinking stock market caused US families to lose $16 trillion.[9]

The collapsing economy also resulted in job loss. By late 2008, 600,000 jobs were being lost every month.[10] In December 2007, the unemployment rate was at 5 percent. By January 2009, it was at 7.8 percent. Unemployment was at its worst in October 2009, when it peaked at 10.1 percent.[11]

Although the October 2009 unemployment rate suggests otherwise, according to the National Bureau of Economic Research, the Great Recession officially ended in June 2009. That is when businesses hit a low point and then began to improve. The financial situation began to improve for many, but the damage that had been done continued into the 2010s. Barnes summed up the general result of the economic catastrophe: "When the credit bubble burst in 2008, so did the accompanying illusions. All this is a tragedy not just for hard-hit families but also for the idea of America as a nation of self-reliant citizens."[13]

DISCUSSION STARTERS

- Did the Great Recession have an impact on the lives of your family members? How did it affect them?

- How do you think the internet has affected the middle class in the United States? How might it continue to change things in the future?

- Was Reaganomics successful? Explain your answer.

FIVE

A SHIFT IN THE
MIDDLE CLASS

A merica's middle class is changing in multiple ways. Since 1970, the number of people in the middle class has decreased each decade. By 2015, the middle class stopped being the majority group in the United States. Instead, the rich and the poor, the groups above and below the middle class, made up half of the US population.

Shifting levels of education have had an effect, too. Pew compared data from 1971 and 2015. The research group divided education level into four groups, with the highest group having at least a bachelor's degree. It found that there were fewer people in the middle class at all levels of education. Pew also found an increase in the number of people at the poverty

Middle-class families now make up a smaller proportion of the country's population than they have in decades.

level, including for people with a bachelor's degree. In 1971, 8 percent of lower-income Americans had a minimum of a four-year degree. In 2015, this figure was 12 percent.[1] This suggests that, more than ever, having a bachelor's degree does not guarantee a person will advance to middle-class status.

MULTIPLE MIDDLE CLASSES

The middle class is also experiencing divisions within itself. Economists identify three subclasses within the middle class. They are the upper middle class, the middle middle class, and the lower middle class. As with most class-based definitions of these kinds, the income ranges for these subclasses vary. The different cutoff points depend on the person or organization that is doing the classifying.

SHARES OF HOUSEHOLD INCOME, 1970–2015[2]

The income gap in the United States becomes apparent when looking at how the overall income totals are distributed. By 2015, the lowest-earning fifth of Americans earned 3.1 percent of the total income. The highest-earning fifth took home 51.1 percent of the income. This gap has persisted and even worsened over the last few decades.

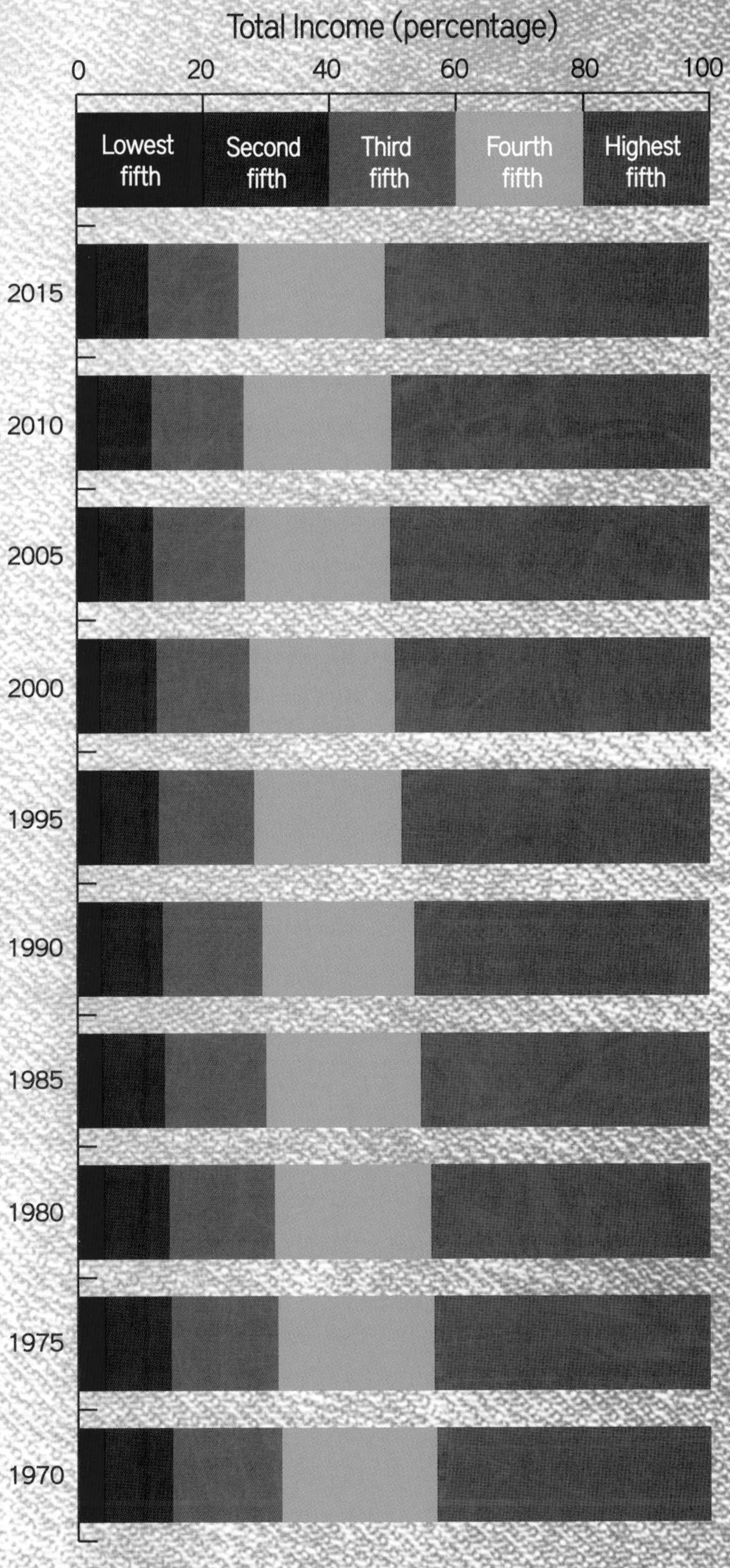

Total Income (percentage)

0   20   40   60   80   100

| | Lowest fifth | Second fifth | Third fifth | Fourth fifth | Highest fifth |

2015

2010

2005

2000

1995

1990

1985

1980

1975

1970

The Urban Institute defines the upper middle class as a household of three people earning between $100,000 and $350,000 per year.[3] It gives the income range of the middle middle class as between $30,000 and $100,000 per year. Pew's numbers for this group are slightly different at from $37,666 to $113,000.[4] The lower middle class earns the least amount of money among these subclasses. The members of this group are above the poverty level, but not by much. The Brookings Institution has defined lower middle class for a family of three as earning between $18,871 and $47,177 per year.[5]

AN ECONOMIC GAP

A gap exists between the middle and upper classes, and it has been growing. In 1983, wealthy families had an average of three times as much wealth as middle-class families. Thirty years later, in 2013, upper-class families had seven times as much.[6] This gap includes the upper middle class, which is separating from the middle class and heading toward becoming part of the upper class. The upper middle class has grown. From 1979 to 2014, it more than doubled, increasing from 12.9 percent of the US population to 29.4 percent.[7]

Nathan Joo and Richard V. Reeves of the Brookings Institution wrote about the upper middle class and this difference in earnings growth:

The idea that the real divide is between ordinary members of the bottom 99% and the rich 1% is a dangerous one, since it makes it easier for those in the upper middle class to convince themselves they are in the same economic boat as the rest of America; they're not.[8]

Since 1971, the social classes have been shifting. There has been significant economic gain, but the new wealth has not benefited all Americans equally. The middle class has been left behind or is lagging. The amount of income going to the upper class has grown dramatically, increasing from 29 percent in 1970 to 49 percent in 2014. By contrast, the amount going to the middle class decreased from 62 percent to 43 percent during this same time.[9]

The percentage of Americans who are part of the middle class is shrinking. The middle class dropped from 61 percent of Americans in 1971 to 50 percent in 2015. In December 2015, Pew released the report "The American Middle Class Is Losing Ground." Pew researchers analyzed data from the US Census

Bureau and found that the middle class is no longer the majority in the United States. For decades, the number of people in the middle class was greater than the total number of Americans in the upper and lower classes. In 2015, the numbers were almost the same, with the combination of the upper and lower populations passing the middle class by 500,000.[11]

The shrinking of the middle class is not necessarily a bad thing for all of those leaving it. Most of those who are no longer part of the middle class have moved up. Two-thirds of middle-class Americans earn enough income to have advanced into the status of the rich. The remaining third, however, have moved in the opposite direction, sinking to a lower level.

LEAVING THE MIDDLE CLASS

In April 2017, CBS News listed signs to identify that one is no longer in the middle class. It suggested that if a household's income goes below $35,300 or rises above $105,881, that family has left the middle class. Another sign was an increase in the available amount of disposable income. Finally, it suggested that if people find themselves not worried about the cost of health care, they are no longer middle class.

PERCEPTIONS OF THE MIDDLE CLASS TODAY

As the middle class has shifted in recent years, so has the way many Americans view it in terms of lifestyle. In its series "The New Middle," NPR's program *All Things Considered* asked listeners which material goods they identify as being part of the middle-class lifestyle today.

Tony Crane called in from Washington and gave a general sense of what the new middle class means. Focusing on expenses, he said, "The new middle is when your tax, rent, food and transportation costs slowly increase while your savings decrease." Michigan's Brittany Hall highlighted getting by and being OK. She responded by saying, "It's having all generic everything, even most medication and always being on the financial edge but somehow still being happy." Emily Wah of Montana presented the most detailed idea of the new middle class: "The new middle should mean a roof over your head, reliable car, healthy food, college, retirement—bonus points if you can take the occasional vacation without completely breaking the bank. Here's a secret. It doesn't."[12]

THE DANGERS OF A GREAT DIVIDE

In *Liberty and Dividends for All*, journalist Peter Barnes discusses the great disparity that has grown between the upper and middle classes. He notes several negative effects of such unequal distribution of wealth:

> As studies have shown, highly unequal societies have more homicides, obesity, heart disease, mental illness, drug abuse, infant mortality, and teenage pregnancies than do more egalitarian societies. Highly unequal societies also suffer from a loss of spirit. When people know their economic system is stacked against them, they cease to believe they can attain security and comfort, much less riches. They also lose faith in their political system, which, mirroring their economy, makes a mockery of the American vision.[13]

Studies conducted in the 2010s show that having vacation money is important to being thought of as middle class, but other factors were more important. The television network ABC asked respondents in 2010 if they thought five specific factors were essential to being considered middle class. The factors were owning a home, being able to save money, being able to spend money on things that aren't critical needs, having money for vacations, and being able to buy a new car. Researchers at the University of Connecticut conducted the same poll in 2013. At least 60 percent of respondents in both polls thought all five factors were indicators of being middle class. In both polls, being able to own a home and being able to save money were the top two choices.

As many middle-class Americans adjusted to a decline in their living situations, polls found people's perceptions of the middle class were declining, too. In early 2015, the CBS television network reported that a large majority of Americans, 71 percent, believed life for middle-class Americans had gotten worse over the last decade.[14]

DISCUSSION STARTERS

- How does the shrinking of the middle class affect US culture and society?

- Why do you think unequal wealth distribution leads to so many negative effects?

SIX

STRUGGLING
TO GET BY

Almost ten years after the beginning of the Great Recession, many Americans are still struggling, especially those in the middle class. Based on median income, the US middle class was the richest in the world for decades, but that is no longer true. In 2015, Canada's middle class took the top spot.

In July 2017, the insurance and finance company Country Financial revealed the results of a survey of 1,000 adult Americans. The study focused on respondents' recoveries from the Great Recession. It showed that African Americans, low-income people, and women had suffered the most financially. At least 25 percent of respondents in each of these

For many families that consider themselves middle class, financial stress has become a part of everyday life.

WISCONSIN'S GREAT MIDDLE-CLASS DECLINE

From 2000 to 2013, the number of middle-class households decreased in every state. Wisconsin experienced the greatest shift, dropping from 55 percent to 49 percent. Household income decreased by 14 percent.

Job loss likely played a major role. A large part of Wisconsin's economy is manufacturing. Since 2000, the number of manufacturing jobs dropped by as much as 20 percent. Marc Levine, director of the University of Wisconsin–Milwaukee Center for Economic Development, explained, "Manufacturing jobs aren't paying what they used to anymore, and a big chunk of that is because of the de-unionization that has occurred."[3] Fewer Americans, including Wisconsinites, belong to unions, organizations of workers that collectively negotiate with companies. Also, many people who worked in manufacturing are now in the service industry, earning less than they had been making.

groups said they still would not be able to pay their bills within one month of losing their jobs.[1]

However, the survey also included some positive elements. A majority of Americans, almost 67 percent, were confident they had power over their financial well-being and recovery. Country Financial's chief marketing officer, Doyle Williams, said of this response, "In light of all the world's uncertainty, this self-reliance that Americans still feel, like 'individually I have the most control over what happens to me,' that was a very optimistic and uplifting note that came out of the survey."[2] But even with such optimism, being a member of the middle class no longer has the sense of security it once did. In fact, many middle-class Americans today have the opposite experience.

LEARNING FROM 235 HOUSEHOLDS

Researchers Jonathan Morduch and Rachel Schneider wanted to understand the financial world of middle-class Americans. They tracked the finances of 235 households, focusing on homes with at least one person employed. They kept track of all incoming and outgoing money.

The participants varied demographically. They included Asian, Hispanic, black, and white families. Some were newly arrived immigrants, whereas others were from families who had been in the United States for several decades. Participants represented rural and urban areas.

The researchers found two important facts affecting income for the middle-class families they studied. Unreliable work hours and unexpected expenses made getting by extremely difficult. Study participants had inconsistent incomes.

NEAL GABLER'S EXPERIENCE

Author and Public Broadcasting Service (PBS) movie critic Neal Gabler is a middle-class American who, like many, has personally felt the struggle to get by. He shared his experience in "The Secret Shame of Middle-Class Americans," an article for the *Atlantic*: "I know what it is like to have to juggle creditors . . . to be down to my last $5—literally—while I wait for a paycheck to arrive . . . to subsist for days on a diet of eggs . . . to dread going to the mailbox, because there will always be new bills to pay but seldom a check with which to pay them. . . . And I know what it is like to have to borrow money from my adult daughters because my wife and I ran out of heating oil."[4]

When the costs of everyday necessities rise, middle-class families find it harder to stay financially afloat.

On average, their incomes varied 25 percent more or 25 percent less than average for five months out of the year. "In other words," Morduch and Schneider wrote, "incomes were far from average almost half of the time. Income volatility was more extreme for poorer families, but middle class families felt it too."[5] Inconsistent wages resulted from inconsistent, unpredictable work hours. Having a job with tips or that relied on commissions also played a role. Participants' desire for a steady income was strong. They indicated in a survey that they would rather have a more reliable income than a higher one.

Another statistic also illustrated the participants' struggle to get by. Almost 40 percent of participating families reported not being able to pay for a $500 emergency, such as a necessary car repair, on their own.

egular 429 9/10

ius 444 9/10

remium
iesel 499 9/10

Instead, the family would have to rely on family or friends to pay for the expense.

Schneider spoke about what she and Morduch learned: "Many people who are middle class nevertheless have the experience of being poor over the course of the year." According to her, middle-class Americans have many worries, including paying for everyday necessities such as food, gas, and utilities. Morduch and Schneider wrote about their findings:

> Families bear far more economic risk than they have in the past. Their jobs deliver less-steady income, even when they are full-time. They have less room between their incomes and their spending needs, and less ability to accumulate reserves. And employers and government do less to buffer individual families from the resulting ups and downs.[6]

GOING WITHOUT HEALTH INSURANCE

The cost of health care has been a growing concern for middle-class Americans. Overall, the amount of spending by Americans on health care has been leveling out in recent years, rather than continuing to grow, as it had been. However, the amount of money spent on health care by middle-class Americans has been going up.

In 2017, middle-class Americans spent more on health-care expenses than families in other classes. Poor individuals or families often qualify to receive Medicaid. At the other end of the spectrum, wealthy Americans have the finances to pay for their health-care needs. They also often have high-quality health insurance through their jobs. The challenge for many middle-class Americans is being in a position between these two extremes. They make too much money to qualify for assistance or subsidies, but they do not make enough money to afford the rising costs.

During his time as president of the United States, Barack Obama made health care a priority. He wanted all Americans to have health insurance. The result was the Affordable Care Act (ACA), which people commonly refer to as Obamacare.

OBAMA'S TASK FORCE

Some of the top politicians in the United States have acknowledged the struggles facing a large portion of the US population. On January 30, 2009, President Barack Obama created a task force to study middle-class families. Vice President Joe Biden led the project. Biden spoke about the task force during a press conference for its launch, saying, "America's middle class is hurting. . . . It is our charge to get the middle class—the backbone of this country—up and running again."[7]

The task force released an annual report in February 2010. The document addressed many topics, including work, retirement, and advancing into the middle class. The task force ended the 43-page report with information many middle-class Americans already knew:

> The challenges facing the middle class took many years to develop, and they will take time to address. The American economy is beginning to pull out of this deep recession, but as the economy returns to growth, the middle class must not be left behind again.[8]

Obamacare had two important features. First, it required everyone to have insurance. This was known as the individual mandate. People who did not have health insurance had to pay a penalty when they filed their federal taxes. The amount of the penalty varied. For adults in 2016 and 2017, it was 2.5 percent of household income or $695, whichever amount was higher.[9]

Second, the law made covering preexisting conditions a requirement. Sometimes, an insurance company would deny coverage to someone who has or has had a medical condition. Obamacare ended that practice. It also stopped health insurers

With health-care costs critically important to middle-class families, debates over health insurance reform have become heated in recent years.

from denying coverage or raising the cost of insurance for a person already covered if they get sick. Requiring everyone to have insurance was meant to help health insurers cover these additional costs.

Many Americans receive health insurance as an employment benefit, but many others find and pay for their own health-care plans. The benefit of Obamacare for these Americans is that the law kept insurance companies from charging higher rates to people with an illness.

In November 2016, officials said the cost for health care was expected to continue rising sharply. People who qualify for subsidies would not feel some of the increase because those subsidies would also go up. But for some middle-class Americans who do not qualify for subsidies, health insurance could become unaffordable.

Lindsay Travnicek is one of those people. Travnicek lives in Arizona, where she works as a dietitian. She is self-employed and pays the entire cost of her health insurance herself. In 2016, she paid $255 a month and had a deductible of $2,000. After the increase, her health insurance plan would cost $430 per month with a deductible of $4,200.

Travnicek had to decide if she would pay the higher rate. She told NPR that she was going to stop her health insurance: "I feel like I'm getting the short end of the stick. You know, I've paid into the system a long time as a healthy person. And I just am choosing not to pay anymore."[10] The decision was not easy for Travnicek, but she felt that in her financial position, it was the only option.

In 2017, Obamacare was on the chopping block. President Donald Trump and the Republican Party had long promised to repeal the law. Their efforts to do so in the spring and summer of 2017 fizzled out. But regardless of the fate of the ACA, middle-class Americans were already suffering, as journalist John Tozzi wrote for *Bloomberg Businessweek* in July 2017:

Whatever happens to Obamacare in Washington, the rest of America will be left with a problem it's had for decades: Health-care spending is growing at an unsustainable rate. Insurance and medical costs are draining the incomes of the middle class—tens of millions of people who earn too much to qualify for government-subsidized coverage, but not so much that they don't feel the bite of medical bills—and nothing on Congress's agenda is likely to fix that.[12]

The individual mandate was repealed as part of a sweeping tax reform bill signed into law in late 2017 by President Trump. Trump and Republicans in Congress declared this would help destroy the ACA. Experts watched to see what effect this would have on the health insurance market.

NOT SAVING FOR RETIREMENT

A characteristic often associated with the middle class has been saving for retirement. But today, many Americans, including those in the middle class, are not setting aside money for later in life. According to the Economic Policy Institute (EPI), almost half of US families have saved nothing for retirement. And most of those who have are wealthy. The EPI found that nine in ten families whose household incomes fell in the top 20 percent had retirement savings. Just one in ten of the lowest 20 percent did.[13]

The average retirement savings for families is $95,776, but that number is skewed by the fact that some people have saved much more than this. Many people have little or no retirement savings. The EPI notes that the median retirement savings for all families in the United States is $5,000. In contrast, when removing families with zero retirement savings from the calculation, the median for families with at least some savings is $60,000.

Being able to save for retirement can mean the difference between a comfortable lifestyle and a stressful one.

When analyzing these averages, the researchers pointed out that the disparity between the mean and the median for all families "indicates inequality—that the large account balances of families with the most savings are driving up the average for all families."[14] Many people now expect they will need to rely on their children for financial support in retirement.

PAYING FOR COLLEGE

Attending college has also been commonly associated with the middle class. But today members of the middle class struggle to pay for college. Tuition has risen sharply in recent decades, and middle-class families are less able to afford it. In addition, getting financial aid is not always easy. Simply put, middle-class Americans are too poor

Protesters have called attention to the crushing burden that people with student loans can face.

to pay for college and too rich to qualify for the aid they need to make college an option.

Gage Marquez cried when he found out the University of California, San Diego, had accepted him. He wants to be the first member in his family to go to college. He dreams of becoming a doctor. Financial aid was minimal, leaving thousands for Gage and his parents to pay. After four years, Gage would have more than $27,000 in student loans. His parents would have $72,000.[15]

Student loan debt is another financial weight many middle-class Americans face. More than 44 million Americans have student debt, totaling $1.3 trillion. The national student loan debt increased by $31 billion in the last quarter of 2016 alone. Students in the class of 2016 averaged $37,172 in student loan debt. More than two million borrowers owe more than $100,000, and more than 400,000 borrowers owe more than $200,000. With such high debt, many borrowers fall behind in making payments. More than 11 percent of borrowers are behind on their payments. The amount of loan debt in seriously delinquent status, which means it's 90 days or more behind in payment, is $31 billion.[16] Neil Swidey reported on college debt for the *Boston Globe* in 2016, writing, "We tell students they need a bachelor's degree to get ahead. But for too many, the numbers no longer add up."[17]

DISCUSSION STARTERS

- Some people have proposed making some or all college free. What is your opinion on this proposal? How might it affect the middle class?

- What do you think about President Obama's task force that studied the middle class? Was it a good project? Why or why not?

- Many middle-class Americans do not have retirement savings. What do you think about that? Is saving important? Why or why not?

GAPS IN THE
MIDDLE CLASS

A merican culture has long held strong the idea of the nation being a meritocracy. This is the idea of the American dream—that if a person is talented, hardworking, and dedicated, that person will succeed and even advance in terms of social class. In other words, a person is rewarded based on his or her merit. Believing in meritocracy can offer hope. Darren Walker, president of the Ford Foundation, spoke about the idea: "As Americans, we want to believe that you can get on that mobility escalator and ride it as far as you want, but that no one rides it faster than anyone else."[1]

However, many experts argue that the idea of meritocracy in the United States is a myth. The journey to success and

The American dream may feel out of reach for people living in neighborhoods where homes are knocked down, boarded up, or abandoned.

Differences in pay across gender and racial lines can contribute to significant disparities in overall wealth.

upward mobility is much quicker for some people than others. The divide is often by race, with white people achieving more and getting there faster. US society has a racial hierarchy, including in its economic system. Gender has also been a major factor in a person's economic success.

MEDIAN INCOME BY RACE AND GENDER

The overall median household income in the United States was $59,039 in 2016. However, the US Census also tracks the median household income by race. This analysis revealed a wide range, with a difference of more than $40,000 between the highest and lowest earners. The figure for Asian households was $81,431. Next came non-Hispanic white households ($65,041), followed by

Hispanic households ($47,675) and African American households ($39,490).[2]

Wealth also varies by race. And the differences are even greater than those in income. In 2015, Latino households had only 8 percent of the wealth of white households, and African American households had 6 percent. Wealth is important because it gives a person or family economic security. But wealth disparity can have significant effects. Catherine Ruetschlin works for Demos, an organization that supports democracy and equality. She cowrote the report "The Racial Wealth Gap: Why Policy Matters," and she explained, "Huge subsets of the population are excluded from accessing the avenues toward wealth. . . . Wealth inequality means, when the economy hits [an uncertain] patch, people don't have the resources to withstand those shocks."[3]

Regarding income, the Census Bureau provided figures broken out based on gender, too. In 2016, the median annual income for men was $10,000 more than for women. Massachusetts Institute of Technology economics professor Peter Temin discussed in his book *The Vanishing Middle Class* that women continue to struggle with prejudice in the workplace. According to Temin, women earn approximately 20 percent less than men, and that difference persists even when women attain high statuses in their fields. The cause of the disparity is unknown. Temin explained, "Scholars are actively seeking to understand the source of this wage gap, but it shows up even after correcting for observable differences."[4]

THE AFRICAN-AMERICAN MIDDLE CLASS

Class varies widely in terms of income, and the experiences Americans have can vary greatly by race. Most notably, African Americans in general are not doing as well as whites. African Americans are the group least likely to be part of the upper class and most likely to have lower-than-average incomes.

Beyond these general differences, African Americans have unequal experiences in specific areas. Richard V. Reeves and Dayna Bowen Matthew have studied the middle class and race. They found several gaps between middle-class Americans who are African American and those who are white.

LIVING ON THE MARGIN IN HOUSTON

In August 2017, Hurricane Harvey caused flooding in Houston, Texas. Residents of the city's east side suffered from more than floodwaters. The neighborhoods in this area are located next to petrochemical plants, oil refineries, and shipping lanes. The floodwaters brought pollution, including toxic waste. Robert Bullard, a sociologist at Texas Southern University, explained, "The people who are generally going to get left out are individuals on the margin, who may own a house, but may not have flood insurance or may not have a cushion or savings account to weather the storm until they get their insurance."[5]

RACIAL GAPS

Infant mortality is one area with a big gap, and the number is not solely related to poverty. The rate of infant mortality is higher for middle-class African Americans than it is for lower-class whites.

Tragic disparities exist in infant mortality rates among whites and African Americans.

Analyzing the numbers by education level reveals a dramatic disparity. The infant death rate for blacks was more than twice that for whites, even at the highest education level. Data from the Centers for Disease Control and Prevention for 2007 through 2013 show that a baby born to a highly educated black woman was more likely to die during its first year of life than a baby born to a white woman with an eighth grade education or lower.[6] Researchers believe that at least some of this discrepancy is due to racial discrimination against mothers, which can have an impact on the physical health of a pregnant woman and her baby.

Another difference for college-educated black women regards marital status. Reeves and Matthew found a marriage gap. Americans with more income and more education tend to get married and stay married. This is not the case for some African Americans. Black women who have a college degree are less likely to marry than white women with a college degree. Sixty percent of African American women ages 25 to 35 who have a college degree have never been married. The percentage of similar white women is 38.[7]

College debt is another area with a racial gap. Earning a college degree can play an important role in increasing income and, as a result, moving upward in class. For many Americans who earn a bachelor's degree, student loan debt is a part of life and often a challenging one. The issue is even greater for African

Americans. Four years after finishing college, the average student loan debt for whites was $28,006. For blacks, it was $52,726.[8]

An examination of neighborhoods revealed more differences. When comparing native-born black Americans with native-born black British citizens, data show that neighborhood segregation in cities was almost triple for the Americans than for the British. (Native-born people were studied because immigrants tend to settle in groups together, which could skew the numbers.) The situation is linked to income. African Americans are more likely to be poor and to live in poor neighborhoods than white Americans. Data show that 9 percent of the residents of poor neighborhoods are white and 37 percent are African American.

But segregation is not limited to lower-class Americans. For blacks, it reaches well into higher incomes. Among families earning more than $100,000 annually, African Americans are four times as likely as whites to live in poor neighborhoods. In addition, half as many of these wealthy black families live in affluent areas as their white counterparts.[9]

African Americans also experience a disparity in school quality. Middle-class black families often live in neighborhoods where school performance is below average. Given that black families tend to be poorer than white families and live in poorer neighborhoods, this statistic is not surprising. That is because schools in poorer neighborhoods tend to be not as good as

school board on unequal funding. The students have also created a classroom library dedicated to books by African American and Latino writers, and they worked to get a new playground installed. The kids saw the gaps in their school and fought to close them in ways meaningful to them.

DISCUSSION STARTERS

- What do you think about the idea of meritocracy? Do you think people who work harder will do better in life?

- Have you ever seen or experienced one of the gaps described in the chapter? Explain.

- What disparities have you seen in your school or neighborhood? What can you do to fight or limit such gaps?

EIGHT

LOOKING
AHEAD

The American middle class has been struggling and continues to face difficulties. The situation has no clearly foreseeable end. But many people have proposed solutions to improve the lives of people in America's middle class.

SAVING THE MIDDLE CLASS

Doyle Williams, chief marketing officer for Country Financial, noted that a gap in job skills is a factor in the slow recovery: "The challenge is that people are either locked into areas where there's no job opportunity . . . or don't have job skills." And many Americans are worried about work. One-third of respondents to a Country Financial survey indicated the job market is the main

Protestors and activists have urged politicians to enact policies to help restore the nation's middle class.

issue affecting their financial security. Williams advocated for new jobs to improve people's finances:

> Ten years ago, the housing crisis was the most important thing. Now that crisis has passed. For most people, home values have risen, so that's no longer the most important issue. Now it's about how to improve the personal finance situation—with jobs.[1]

Dan Schawbel, research director at Future Workplace, explained that millions of jobs are in need of workers in the United States, but people with the right skills are not available. Schawbel offered a solution:

DIVIDENDS FOR ALL

Journalist Peter Barnes wants to help the middle class. Barnes wrote his 2014 book, *With Liberty and Dividends for All*, because he is "appalled by the decline of America's middle class and outraged when our leaders mislead us about what we can and can't do to stop it." Barnes believes the solution to helping middle-class Americans lies in giving them more than just jobs. The nation needs to create income unrelated to jobs and not through taxes. He thinks the key is "dividends from wealth we own together."[2] Each legal resident would get the same amount and receive the payment electronically. And the money would exist as long as the economy was doing well. Alaska residents benefit from such a program. The Alaska Permanent Fund is an account into which the state places at least 25 percent of its earnings from Alaskan oil drilling. Each year, every Alaska resident gets an equal share of money earned by that fund. In 2015, the dividend was more than $2,000. For a family of four, that was income totaling more than $8,000.[3] For Americans in the middle and lower classes, such a dividend could be an important source of income.

Companies need to do a better job of examining the skills they need and then incorporating the right training to get their employees up to speed. By up-skilling your employees, they are able to shift into more in-demand, critical positions in your company, which allows you to compete at a higher level.[4]

STRENGTHEN SOCIAL SECURITY

Senator Bernie Sanders of Vermont believes one way to help middle-class Americans is by strengthening Social Security. In August 2015, Sanders wrote an article for the Senior Citizens League. He discussed a situation facing many middle-class Americans: "Millions of middle-class Americans face a looming retirement crisis as a result of growing wealth inequality."

Sanders addressed the importance of Social Security to seniors, citizens with disabilities, and children whose parents have died. He wrote that the average monthly benefit to seniors of $1,328 was insufficient to keep someone in the middle class. To improve the situation, Sanders suggested strengthening Social Security. In 2016, the highest amount of earnings that would be taxed for Social Security was $118,500. This means that someone who earns $18 million per year pays the same amount of payroll taxes as someone who earns $118,500 per year. Sanders suggested increasing taxes on the wealthy. Sanders explained, "It's time to address our real problems—growing inequality and our looming retirement crisis."[5] According to the senator, his plan would extend Social Security's reserves for 50 years and support an increase in seniors' benefits to help them afford an increased cost of living.

EXPECTATIONS

Many researchers have analyzed the middle class in recent years, exploring changes in income and how people identify this group. The companies Allstate and National Journal polled Americans about realistic expectations, asking them to rank items as realistic for almost anyone, the middle class and up, or only the upper class to obtain. The items included paying for children's college education, saving enough for retirement, being able to pay bills without going into debt, and owning a home.

Owning a home scored highest, with 61 percent of respondents stating they believed middle-class Americans

BERNIE SANDERS'S SPEECH

On December 10, 2010, members of the US Senate had before them a plan to cut taxes amounting to $858 billion.[6] The plan benefited wealthy Americans. Senator Bernie Sanders of Vermont disagreed with the plan, so he spoke out against it for 8 hours and 35 minutes.

Sanders had not planned to speak that long, but he was passionate about the topic: "It was an opportunity to . . . really talk about why the middle class of this country is collapsing, why the gap between the very rich and everybody else is going—growing wider and why many, many people in this country are worried about our future and what happens to their kids." Even with his speech, the Senate passed the bill and President Obama soon signed it into law.[7]

could realistically expect to achieve this milestone. Less than half of respondents believed all the remaining items were realistic expectations. Forty-four percent of those polled said being able to afford a yearly vacation, being able to afford good health care, and being able to pay bills without going into debt were realistic for middle-class Americans. Even fewer believed having money to cope with unemployment or a health emergency, having job security, and getting regular raises were realistic expectations.[8]

THE EFFECTS OF ECONOMIC HARDSHIP ON CHILDREN

Researchers at Princeton University and Columbia University have been conducting a long-term study of more than 5,000 children and their parents. The Fragile Families and Child Wellbeing Study began in 1998. After the Great Recession, researchers at Columbia used data from the study to understand nine-year-olds affected by the financial downturn. Many of the children in the study lived in single-parent households, which put the families more at risk for financial struggle. Because the data come from the long-term study, study authors had information about the participants from before and after the Great Recession hit. The Columbia researchers learned that children, especially boys, have an increased risk of both emotional and behavioral issues as a result of economic hardship. Many coped through vandalism and drinking or taking drugs.

Psychologist Romeo Vitelli wrote about the study for *Psychology Today*, noting its importance: "While the worst of the Great Recession may have passed, its legacy still continues. As well, new economic downturns will cause further hardship in [the] future and children, who are more vulnerable than most people realize, will face the worst of it. Even for those children not living in poverty, economic uncertainty poses risks that are only beginning to be appreciated. Being aware of these risks and the different ways that parents can help protect their children can be essential to avoid long-term problems."[9]

President Donald Trump urged Congress to enact large tax cuts in the fall of 2017.

The ideal that had long been the American middle class had eroded in reality, leaving Americans with few expectations for this once strong segment of America's social fabric.

THE 2017 TAX BILL

In the fall of 2017, the Republican Party turned its focus to new legislation that would make significant changes to the nation's tax laws. The party controlled the presidency and both houses of Congress, meaning it had the opportunity to make many changes it desired without relying on Democratic votes. In general, the Republicans sought to lower taxes on most Americans. By far the largest cuts would go to corporations. Republicans argued that by lowering these tax rates, those corporations would have more money to spend on hiring and raising wages.

Senators and representatives argued over the details, but eventually they came to a final agreement. President Trump signed the legislation, officially called the Tax Cuts and Jobs Act, on December 22. In the final bill, tax cuts for individuals were set to expire in 2025. The tax cuts for corporations were made permanent. Critics argued that the legislation represented a major benefit for corporations at the expense of poor and middle-class Americans. They also pointed out that the enormous tax cuts would significantly lower the government's revenue, raising the national debt. In response, Republicans argued that by boosting the economy, the cuts would offset the lowered revenue. As the cuts took effect in 2018, people around the country watched closely to see what effect the sweeping changes would have on the middle class.

BRIDGING THE DUAL ECONOMY

Peter Temin, a professor of economics at the Massachusetts Institute of Technology, says, "We have a fractured society. The middle class is vanishing." Temin describes the US economy as a dual economy divided between rich and poor. The upper level is the finance, technology, and electronics (FTE) sector. The lower level is the low-wage sector. Low-wage jobs include cleaning, customer service, and food service. Those in the FTE sector usually do well. Those in the low-wage sector tend to have a difficult time. Temin believes education is a key factor in improving the situation for those in the lower sector: "The link between the two parts of the modern dual economy is education, which provides a possible path that children of low-wage workers can take to move into the FTE sector."[10] This education begins in early childhood and continues through college.

WHY THE MIDDLE CLASS IS IMPORTANT

As the middle class continues to cope with its worsening conditions, a variety of experts have had thoughts about what to do to make things better for Americans, including the middle class. At least one author wrote about why the country needs a middle class. Lincoln Mitchell, a writer on political development, wrote about the middle class in 2010, in the midst of the Great Recession. He closed his piece with this thought:

If the middle class in the US continues to wither away due to recession, constant unemployment, government policies that are not supportive of middle class Americans and that outsource jobs overseas, it will not just be formerly middle class Americans who will suffer, it will also be difficult for American society and democracy to hold together. A large and stable middle class has been central to America's wealth and stability for decades; without this middle class the country's future will be in great peril.[11]

Experts know what is causing the middle class to shrink. Knowing the cause is half the battle to resolving the issue. Eliminating achievement gaps, reducing income inequality, and ensuring that Americans are ready to take on the jobs of the future are three methods that experts have identified for helping strengthen the middle class. This information can guide leaders to make changes to help middle-class Americans. With the right plans, middle-class Americans can do more than survive; they can thrive. The history of the United States suggests that a strong middle class will result in benefits to the entire nation.

DISCUSSION STARTERS

- What do you think the future holds for middle-class Americans?

- Do you think strengthening Social Security is important? Explain.

- From what you have learned, what do you think might help the middle class? Do you think helping the middle class is important? Why or why not?

ESSENTIAL FACTS

SIGNIFICANT EVENTS

- The GI Bill helped create the middle class in the years immediately following World War II. Federal money available to military veterans allowed them the opportunity to buy homes to create what became the middle-class lifestyle. The GI Bill helped many Americans achieve the American dream, but not all US veterans benefited from it. Blacks and other minorities were denied the chance to even apply for a loan to live in some areas, such as Levittown, New York, the first suburban development.

- Reaganomics tax cuts for businesses and the wealthy in the early 1980s were meant to trickle down to all Americans, but that did not happen. During this time, average wages did not grow and sometimes decreased, even as productivity grew. Only 5 percent of workers had enough gains to outpace the rate of inflation, and they were mostly among the top one percent of earners. This worsened the existing gap between the wealthy and the middle and lower classes.

- A credit crisis and housing bubble led to the Great Recession in 2007. The economy collapsed, which resulted in dramatic stock market losses and unemployment. The Great Recession officially ended in June 2009, but Americans continued to struggle financially into the 2010s.

- Since the 1960s, upper-class incomes have grown at a faster rate than middle-class incomes, which has created an income gap. And the middle class has decreased in size since the 1970s, dropping from 61 percent of the population in 1971 to approximately 50 percent in 2017.

KEY PLAYERS

- William Levitt developed the first subdivision, launching the move to suburbia.

- Ronald Reagan lowered taxes on businesses and the wealthy to stimulate economic growth and ultimately help all Americans, but that idea of a trickle-down economy did not happen.

- The US Census Bureau tracks income and other data about Americans.

- The Pew Research Center analyzes US Census Bureau data to help people understand economic trends, including the decline of the American middle class.

- Vice President Joe Biden led a task force on the middle class for the Obama administration.

- Senator Bernie Sanders spoke for 8 hours and 35 minutes on December 10, 2010, against planned tax cuts that would benefit wealthy Americans.

IMPACT ON SOCIETY

The American middle class has been critical to US society. For many people, it is the heart of the United States. The middle class has come to represent the American dream aspired to by citizens and immigrants alike. However, for many Americans in the middle class and below, the American dream is only a dream. The issues the people in these classes have faced over the last few decades have left millions of citizens struggling to get by and wondering what the future holds for them. The problems have often been especially severe for women and people of color.

QUOTE

"The challenges facing the middle class took many years to develop, and they will take time to address. The American economy is beginning to pull out of this deep recession, but as the economy returns to growth, the middle class must not be left behind again."

—*Annual Report of the White House Task Force on the Middle Class, 2010*

GLOSSARY

COMMISSION
Money someone earns for making a sale.

CONSUMPTION
The process of consuming, or using.

COST OF LIVING
The amount of money needed to live at a particular standard of well-being.

DEDUCTIBLE
The amount of money a person has to pay for medical expenses before his or her health insurance company begins to help pay for costs.

DISPOSABLE INCOME
Money left over after paying for necessities.

DIVIDEND
A regular payment made by a company or other entity, divided among many people.

HOUSEHOLD
A group of people, related or unrelated, who live at the same address.

INFLATION
An increase in the price of goods and services.

NET WORTH
Money one has after subtracting all of what one owes from all of what one has.

PENSION
Money a company pays to an employee in regular installments after he or she retires; the amount is based on how long the person worked.

PUBLIC HOUSING
Housing the government owns, operates, or sponsors that has low rent.

SOCIAL SECURITY
A US program started in the 1930s to provide retirement income for people over the age of 65.

SUBDIVISION
A large piece of land divided into smaller lots for the purpose of selling them so that homes can be built on them.

TIP
Money given to a worker for a service he or she provided or will provide.

WEALTH
All the items of economic value someone has, such as money and property.

ADDITIONAL
RESOURCES

SELECTED BIBLIOGRAPHY

"A Brief History of America's Middle Class." *NPR*. NPR, 5 July 2016. Web.
9 Oct. 2017.

Barnes, Peter. *With Liberty and Dividends for All*. San Francisco, CA:
Berrett-Koehler, 2014. Print.

Tyler, George R. *What Went Wrong: How the 1% Hijacked the American Middle
Class . . . and What Other Countries Got Right*. Dallas, TX: BenBella, 2013. Print.

FURTHER READINGS

Eboch, M. M. *Race and Economics*. Minneapolis: Abdo, 2018. Print.

Goodwin, Michael and Dan E. Barr. *Economix: How Our Economy Works
(and Doesn't Work), in Words and Pictures*. New York: Abrams ComicArts,
2012. Print.

ONLINE RESOURCES

Booklinks
NONFICTION NETWORK
FREE! ONLINE NONFICTION RESOURCES

To learn more about the American middle class, visit **abdobooklinks.com**.
These links are routinely monitored and updated to provide the most current
information available.

MORE INFORMATION

For more information on this subject, contact or visit the following organizations:

THE LEVITTOWN PROJECT
macamericanstudies.com/courses/levittown

This website, created under the supervision of Professor Duchess Harris and Professor Lizeth Gutierrez, includes information and discussion questions about Levittown, one of the earliest suburban developments in the United States.

NATIONAL MUSEUM OF AMERICAN HISTORY
1300 Constitution Ave. NW
Washington, DC 20560
202-633-1000
americanhistory.si.edu/american-enterprise-exhibition

Explore the American Enterprise Exhibition to learn about the history of business in the United States. The Consumer Era portion of the exhibit covers the 1940s through the 1970s, a time when the middle class focused on buying, including houses in the suburbs.

PEW RESEARCH CENTER
1615 L Street NW, Suite 820
Washington, DC 20036
202-419-4300
pewresearch.org

Pew conducts nonpartisan research in several areas, including US politics, media, science and technology, and demographics.

SOURCE NOTES

CHAPTER 1. THE MIDDLE CLASS NO MORE

1. Ari Shapiro. "Middle Class Earners Struggle to Pay Rent in New York City." *NPR*. NPR, 6 July 2016. Web. 8 Oct. 2017.

2. Shapiro, "Middle Class Earners Struggle to Pay Rent in New York City."

3. Kimberly Amadeo. "What Is Considered Middle Class?" *Balance*. Balance, 30 Aug. 2017. Web. 9 Oct. 2017.

4. "Salaries." *Indeed*. Indeed, 2017. Web. 9 Oct. 2017.

5. Shapiro, "Middle Class Earners Struggle to Pay Rent in New York City."

6. Shapiro, "Middle Class Earners Struggle to Pay Rent in New York City."

7. Tanvi Misra. "The Rise of the Rich Renter." *CityLab*. Atlantic, 5 Oct. 2017. Web. 9 Oct. 2017.

8. Shapiro, "Middle Class Earners Struggle to Pay Rent in New York City."

9. Kathryn Vasel. "These Cities Have the Highest Rents in the Country." *CNN*. CNN, 1 Apr. 2016. Web. 8 Oct. 2017.

10. Kathryn Vasel. "Eleven Million Americans Spend Half Their Income on Rent." *CNN*. CNN, 22 June 2016. Web. 8 Oct. 2017.

11. Hanna Brooks Olsen. "The Absolute Worst Advice We Give to Americans Struggling to Pay Rent." *Daily Dot*. Billboard Music, 11 Dec. 2015. Web. 9 Oct. 2017.

12. Vasel, "Eleven Million Americans Spend Half Their Income on Rent."

13. Shapiro, "Middle Class Earners Struggle to Pay Rent in New York City."

14. John Alden Byrne. "The Rise and the Fall of the American Middle Class." *New York Post*. New York Post, 27 Dec. 2015. Web. 8 Oct. 2017.

15. Amadeo, "What Is Considered Middle Class?"

16. Byrne, "The Rise and the Fall of the American Middle Class."

CHAPTER 2. DEFINING THE MIDDLE CLASS

1. Joao Alhanati. "Which Income Class Are You?" *Investopedia*. Investopedia, 17 Sept. 2017. Web. 17 Sept. 2017.

2. Kimberly Amadeo. "What Is Considered Middle Class?" *Balance*. Balance, 30 Aug. 2017. Web. 9 Oct. 2017.

3. Rebecca Lake. "How Much Income Puts You in the Top 1%, 5%, 10%?" *Investopedia*. Investopedia, 15 Sept. 2016. Web. 23 Jan. 2018.

4. "Income, Poverty, and Health Insurance Coverage in the United States: 2016." *Census*. US Census Bureau, 12 Sept. 2017. Web. 2 Nov. 2017.

5. "The Meaning of Middle Class." *Roper Center*. Roper Center, Cornell University, 2017. Web. 2 Nov. 2017.

6. John Yemma. "A Middle-Class State of Mind." *Christian Science Monitor*. Christian Science Monitor, 2 Nov. 2015. Web. 2 Nov. 2017.

7. Amadeo, "What Is Considered Middle Class?"

8. "Cost of Living: How Far Will My Salary Go in Another City?" *CNN Money*. CNN, n.d. Web. 23 Jan. 2018.

9. Amadeo, "What Is Considered Middle Class?"

10. Amadeo, "What Is Considered Middle Class?"

11. Amadeo, "What Is Considered Middle Class?"

12. "The Meaning of Middle Class."

CHAPTER 3. HISTORY OF THE MIDDLE CLASS

1. James Madison. "Epilogue: Securing the Republic." *University of Chicago*. University of Chicago, 1987. Web. 2 Nov. 2017.

2. Richard Lacayo. "Suburban Legend William Levitt." *Time*. Time, 7 Dec. 1998. Web. 17 Sept. 2017.

3. Paula Span. "Mr. Levitt's Neighborhood." *Washington Post*. Washington Post, 27 May 1997. Web. 30 Oct. 2017.

4. Span, "Mr. Levitt's Neighborhood."

5. Peter Barnes. *With Liberty and Dividends for All*. San Francisco, CA: Berrett-Koehler, 2014. Print. 2.

6. Claire Sudduth. "The Middle Class." *Time*. Time, 27 Feb. 2009. Web. 17 Sept. 2017.

7. Eric Deggans. "Modern Television Portrays Complex View of the Middle Class." *NPR*. NPR, 19 Aug. 2016. Web. 23 Jan. 2018.

8. "Urban Redevelopment." *Encyclopedia.com*. Encyclopedia.com, 2016. Web. 31 Oct. 2017.

9. Robert Powell. "Social Security Is Crucial to the Middle Class." *MarketWatch*. CBS, 22 Aug. 2013. Web. 30 Sept. 2017.

10. "Social Security and People of Color." *National Academy of Social Insurance*. National Academy of Social Insurance, n.d. Web. 29 Oct. 2017.

CHAPTER 4. AN ECONOMIC CHANGE

1. George R. Tyler. *What Went Wrong: How the 1% Hijacked the American Middle Class . . . and What Other Countries Got Right*. Dallas, TX: BenBella, 2013. Print. 3.

2. Tyler, *What Went Wrong*, 3.

3. Tyler, *What Went Wrong*, 4.

4. Tyler, *What Went Wrong*, 5.

5. Tyler, *What Went Wrong*, 10.

6. Tyler, *What Went Wrong*, 19.

7. Tyler, *What Went Wrong*, 13.

8. William H. Davidow. "The Internet Has Been a Colossal Economic Disappointment." *Harvard Business Review*. Harvard, 10 Apr. 2015. Web. 1 Oct. 2017.

9. "Great Recession." *Investopedia*. Investopedia, 2017. Web. 2 Nov. 2017.

10. Michael Levy. "American Recovery and Reinvestment Act." *Encyclopaedia Britannica*. Encyclopaedia Britannica, 27 Apr. 2017. Web. 5 Oct. 2017.

11. Levy, "American Recovery and Reinvestment Act."

12. Levy, "American Recovery and Reinvestment Act."

13. Peter Barnes. *With Liberty and Dividends for All*. San Francisco, CA: Berrett-Koehler, 2014. Print. 20.

CHAPTER 5. A SHIFT IN THE MIDDLE CLASS

1. "A Portrait of America's Middle Class by the Numbers." *NPR*. NPR, 7 July 2016. Web. 7 Oct. 2017.

2. "Historical Income Tables." *US Census Bureau*. US Census Bureau, 10 Aug. 2017. Web. 9 Feb. 2018.

3. Joao Alhanati. "Which Income Class Are You?" *Investopedia*. Investopedia, 17 Sept. 2017. Web. 17 Sept. 2017.

4. Alhanati, "Which Income Class Are You?"

5. Alhanati, "Which Income Class Are You?"

6. "A Portrait of America's Middle Class by the Numbers."

7. Curt Mills. "Upper Middle Class Thriving, Report Says." *US News and World Report*. US News and World Report, 21 June 2016. Web. 9 Feb. 2018.

8. Alhanati, "Which Income Class Are You?"

9. "The American Middle Class Is Losing Ground." *Pew Research Center*. Pew Research Center, 9 Dec. 2015. Web. 2 Nov. 2017.

SOURCE NOTES
CONTINUED

10. Kimberly Amadeo. "What Is the Average American Net Worth?" *Balance*. Balance, 29 May 2017. Web. 22 Sept. 2017.

11. "The American Middle Class Is Losing Ground."

12. "The New Middle: What Material Objects Define the Middle Class in America?" *All Things Considered*. NPR, 9 Aug. 2016. Web. 23 Sept. 2017.

13. Peter Barnes. *With Liberty and Dividends for All*. San Francisco, CA: Berrett-Koehler, 2014. Print. 14.

14. "The Meaning of Middle Class." *Roper Center*. Roper Center, Cornell University, 2017. Web. 2 Nov. 2017.

CHAPTER 6. STRUGGLING TO GET BY

1. Abigail Summerville. "A Decade after Great Recession, One in Three Americans Still Haven't Recovered." *CNBC*. CNBC, 13 July 2017. Web. 9 Oct. 2017.

2. Summerville, "A Decade after Great Recession, One in Three Americans Still Haven't Recovered."

3. Scottie Lee Meyers. "Wisconsin Has Seen Largest Middle-Class Decline of Any State, Study Finds." *Wisconsin Public Radio*. Wisconsin Public Radio, 2 Apr. 2015. Web. 17 Sept. 2017.

4. Neal Gabler. "The Secret Shame of Middle-Class Americans." *Atlantic*. Atlantic, May 2016. Web. 1 Oct. 2017.

5. Jonathan Morduch and Rachel Schneider. "We Tracked Every Dollar 235 US Households Spent for a Year, and Found Widespread Financial Vulnerability." *Harvard Business Review*. Harvard, 12 Apr. 2017. Web. 23 Jan. 2018.

6. Rob Wile. "These 3 Charts Show Why Middle Class Workers Are Struggling to Get Ahead Today." *Time*. Time, 17 Apr. 2017. Web. 23 Jan. 2018.

7. Macon Phillips. "Press Release: Vice President Biden Announces Middle Class Task Force." *White House*. White House, 30 Jan. 2009. Web. 7 Sept. 2017.

8. "Annual Report of the White House Task Force on the Middle Class." *White House*. White House, Feb. 2010. Web. 7 Sept. 2017.

9. "The Fee for Not Having Health Insurance." *HealthCare.gov*. US Centers for Medicare & Medicaid Services, n.d. Web. 30 Oct. 2017.

10. "Middle-Class Americans Face Biggest Strain under Rising Obamacare Costs." *NPR*. NPR, 6 Nov. 2016. Web. 9 Oct. 2017.

11. Annie Nova. "These Charts Show Just How Small the US Middle Class Is, Compared to Europe's." *Time*. Time, 12 June 2017. Web. 8 Oct. 2017.

12. John Tozzi. "With or Without Obamacare, Health-Care Costs Are Battering the Middle Class." *Bloomberg Week*. Bloomberg, 27 July 2017. Web. 2 Nov. 2017.

13. Kathleen Elkins. "Here's How Much the Average American Family Has Saved for Retirement." *CNBC*. CNBC, 12 Sept. 2016. Web. 1 Oct. 2017.

14. Elkins, "Here's How Much the Average American Family Has Saved for Retirement."

15. Katie Lobosco. "Too Poor to Pay for College, Too Rich for Financial Aid." *CNN*. CNN, 29 Apr. 2016. Web. 9 Oct. 2017.

16. Zack Friedman. "Student Loan Debt in 2017: A $1.3 Trillion Crisis." *Forbes*. Forbes, 21 Feb. 2017. Web. 9 Oct. 2017.

17. Neil Swidey. "The College Debt Crisis Is Even Worse Than You Think." *Boston Globe*. Boston Globe, 18 May 2016. Web. 9 Oct. 2017.

CHAPTER 7. GAPS IN THE MIDDLE CLASS

1. Megan Garber. "The Perils of Meritocracy." *Atlantic*. Atlantic, 30 June 2017. Web. 15 Oct. 2017.

2. "Flyover: The Myth of a 'Bootstraps' America." *MPR*. MPR, 17 Sept. 2017. Web. 15 Oct. 2017.

3. Laura Shin. "The Racial Wealth Gap: Why a Typical White Household Has 16 Times the Wealth of a Black One." *Forbes*. Forbes, 26 Mar. 2015. Web. 2 Nov. 2017.

4. Peter Temin. *The Vanishing Middle Class: Prejudice and Power in a Dual Economy*. Cambridge, MA: MIT, 2017. Print. 60.

5. Andrew C. Kaufman. "Houston Flooding Always Hits Poor, Non-White Neighborhoods Hardest." *Huffington Post*. Huffington Post, 29 Aug. 2017. Web. 6 Oct. 2017.

6. Richard V. Reeves and Dayna Bowen Matthew. "Six Charts Showing Race Gaps within the American Middle Class." *Brookings*. Brookings, 21 Oct. 2016. Web. 7 Oct. 2017.

7. Reeves and Matthew, "Six Charts Showing Race Gaps within the American Middle Class."

8. Reeves and Matthew, "Six Charts Showing Race Gaps within the American Middle Class."

9. Reeves and Matthew, "Six Charts Showing Race Gaps within the American Middle Class."

10. Reeves and Matthew, "Six Charts Showing Race Gaps within the American Middle Class."

11. Gillian B. White. "How Black Middle-Class Kids Become Poor Adults." *Atlantic*. Atlantic, 19 Jan. 2015. Web. 6 Oct. 2017.

12. Temin, *The Vanishing Middle Class*, 55.

13. White, "How Black Middle-Class Kids Become Poor Adults."

14. Reeves and Matthew, "Six Charts Showing Race Gaps within the American Middle Class."

15. Melinda D. Anderson. "Why the Myth of Meritocracy Hurts Kids of Color." *Atlantic*. Atlantic, 27 July 2017. Web. 15 Oct. 2017.

CHAPTER 8. LOOKING AHEAD

1. Abigail Summerville. "A Decade after Great Recession, One in Three Americans Still Haven't Recovered." *CNBC*. CNBC, 13 July 2017. Web. 9 Oct. 2017.

2. Peter Barnes. *With Liberty and Dividends for All*. San Francisco, CA: Berrett-Koehler, 2014. Print. xi.

3. Rachel Waldholz. "Alaska's Annual Dividend Adds Up for Residents." *Marketplace*. 16 Mar. 2016. Web. 31 Oct. 2017.

4. Summerville, "A Decade after Great Recession, One in Three Americans Still Haven't Recovered."

5. Bernie Sanders. "Strengthening Social Security to Help Middle-Class Americans." *Senior Citizens League*. Senior Citizens League, 7 Aug. 2015. Web. 30 Sept. 2017.

6. Paul Kane and Felicia Sonmez. "Sen. Bernie Sanders Speaks for Eight Hours against Tax Cuts." *Washington Post*. Washington Post, 11 Dec. 2010. Web. 9 Oct. 2017.

7. "Sen. Bernie Sanders' Eight-Hour Soliloquy." *NPR*. NPR, 16 Dec. 2010. Web. 1 Oct. 2017.

8. "The Meaning of Middle Class." *Roper Center*. Roper Center, Cornell University, 2017. Web. 2 Nov. 2017.

9. Romeo Vitelli. "How Have Children Been Affected by the Great Recession?" *Psychology Today*. Sussex Publishers, 14 Sept. 2015. Web. 3 Oct. 2017.

10. Peter Dizikes. "America's Two-Track Economy." *MIT News*. MIT, 13 Mar. 2017. Web. 15 Oct. 2017.

11. Lincoln Mitchell. "The Middle Class: How We Got One and Why We Need to Keep It." *Huffington Post*. Huffington Post, 25 May 2011. Web. 3 Oct. 2017.

INDEX

ABOUT THE
AUTHORS

DUCHESS HARRIS, JD, PHD

Professor Harris is the chair of the American Studies department at Macalester College and curator of the Duchess Harris Collection of ABDO books. She is the author and coauthor of recently released ABDO books including *Hidden Human Computers: The Black Women of NASA*, *Black Lives Matter*, and *Race and Policing*.

Before working with ABDO, she authored several other books on the topics of race, culture, and American history. She served as an associate editor for *Litigation News*, the American Bar Association Section of Litigation's quarterly flagship publication, and was the first editor in chief of *Law Raza*, an interactive online journal covering race and the law, published at William Mitchell College of Law. She has earned a PhD in American Studies from the University of Minnesota and a JD from William Mitchell College of Law.

REBECCA ROWELL

Rebecca Rowell has put her degree in publishing and writing to work as an editor and as an author, working on dozens of books. Recent topics as an author include Ellis Island and rockets. She lives in Minneapolis, Minnesota.